SUGGESTIONS FOR PERFORMANCE

TOCCATA AND FUGUE IN D MINOR

TOCCATA

The Toccata begins with full organ on the great-manual. It is best to employ the 16-foot manual-stops only for the chords in measures 2, 3, 10, 11, 22, and 27–30, as they would render the runs indistinct and heavy.

Be very careful not to overdo the *Prestissimo* from measures 4 and 22 onward. On the organs for which Bach wrote it, with their deep and heavy touch, this *Prestissimo* could have amounted, at the utmost, to a good modern *allegro*. Neither should the player forget that these runs, taken in too swift a movement, lose the pathetic character on which their effect depends.

There are players who like to perform measures 4–10 on the second manual. This procedure is hardly appropriate, more especially for the reason that it does not allow for a suitable transition from the figurations to the pedal-entrance in measure 10. The second manual should be employed solely for the episode from the last sixteenth in measure 5 to the organ-point in measure 7, this passage being but an echo of the one preceding.

The entrance of the pedal in measure 10 ought, of course, to be prepared by a *rallentando*. The same holds good for measure 27.

During the rest in measure 12 the reeds on all the manuals should be thrown off. In measures 12–15 the right hand plays on the second manual, the left on the third. On a two-manual instrument, the great-organ will have to be transformed into a subsidiary organ by retiring stops; after the first eighth in measure 16 it will be brought up to the normal tone-power.

Measures 12–15 have the best effect when the right-hand part also is played *staccato*, rather than *legato;* the ear can then follow the alto better, between the breaks in the soprano. The lower the range of the soprano descends, the quieter should the tempo be.

From the second eighth in measure 16 on, the great-manual will be used. Some organists like to execute the analogous passages in 32d-notes in measures 16, 17 and 20 on the second manual, not transferring to the great till the second half of each measure, for the sake of the strong contrast. When played thus, however, you run the risk of depriving the 32d-note passages of their grandeur.

It is much better to remain through these measures on the great-manual, and to add stops every time on the eighth where the pedal enters until you arrive, in measure 20, at full organ (without the 16-foot manual-registers). Draw these 16-foot stops for the chord in measure 22, throwing them off again for the following figures in sixteenth-notes. But let them stand from the close of measure 27 on.

From measure 22 until the end, play on the great-manual, and with full organ. However, some organists prefer to reserve a few stops, so as not to reach full organ until measures 26 and 27.

In order that this admirable composition may not have the effect of a chaos, in its majestic disruption, it must be played strictly in time. The *ritenuti*, which seem naturally demanded, must not be exaggerated in the least. A great many players mistakenly imagine that they may permit themselves every liberty and caprice, and act as if they were

31144

playing a rhapsody on the piano. The unity of the fundamental tempo must be preserved.

It will be apparent to every observant organist that the sixteenth-note figurations in measures 4–10 and 22–27 are not simply to be rattled off in triplet-rhythm. Through the triplet-movement let the natural period-form, on which it is based, be clearly perceptible. The motive out of which the figuration grows, reaches over from one triplet-group to the next. Therefore, in measure 4 *et seq.*, play like this:

Measures 8–10 are articulated as follows:

The figures in measures 22–27 will be divided up in this way:

As presented on paper, this phrasing may possibly seem complicated and almost artificial. One might devise groupings which would strike the eye as much more luminous. On comparing them with the foregoing, however, it will be found that no other is equally satisfactory to the ear.

Notice, in particular, that the *rallentandi* which, in measures 10 and 27, lead over to the chords, have the finest effect in the given phrasing. Whereas, at the beginning and in the middle of the figurations, the articulations could only be indicated very discreetly, they will be brought out in increasingly stronger relief as the tempo slows down. Here it is no longer a matter of mere prolongation; there is a feeling as if the note-groups, which till now had been striving against the levelling tendency of the triplet-rhythm wherein they are imbedded, victoriously asserted themselves. They emerge from it, swelling into the towering grandeur immanent to the lofty conception. Thus the *rallentando* becomes the culmination of the entire series of figurations, from out of which the chords are now born.

It is hardly necessary to observe that the ordinary execution of the sixteenth-note triplets allows for no transition from them to the chord, however importunately the *rallentando* may be dwelt on. The last note before the chord—say in measure 27—is, when so executed, already bound up with a preceding accent, and cannot adjust itself to a natural connection with the chord. Even to the eye, this impossibility is evident:

On the other hand, if we phrase according to the fundamental motive of the figures, the final periods in sixteenth-notes assume the form of imposing buttresses to the chord:

FUGUE

The plan of the Fugue is of such grandly simple proportions that most players will probably agree in the main with respect to its registration and the changes of manual to be made.

It begins with foundation stops, on the great-organ. On the second manual (which is coupled to the first) the mixtures may be drawn, from the start, with the foundation stops. These mixtures will hardly be noticeable, as such, while the swell is closed, but they will lend the playing a certain clarity of effect unattainable with foundation stops alone.

A player clad in the armor of sound principles will withstand, in the first principal section, the temptation to fly over now and again to the second manual with the accompanying parts in order to bring out the theme as a solo part on the great, and will confine himself to throwing into relief some few echo-like effects in the accompaniment by a change of manual. We would suggest that in measures 35–38 the third and fourth eighths in the soprano should be regularly executed on the second manual, and also that the last four eighths in each of these measures should be played *staccato*, and the first four eighths *legato*. For this part, however, still other variations in the phrasing and changes of manual may be thought out, whose effect is also good. The sixteenth-notes will, of course, be played *legato*.

In what follows, a good echo-like effect is obtainable by transferring the two inner parts to the second manual from the third quarter in measure 42 to the first in measure 43, from the third quarter in measure 44 to the first in measure 45, and from the fourth eighth in measure 46 to the first quarter in measure 47.

During measures 49 to 51 the swell-box opens, permitting the mixtures of the second manual to assert themselves. By this means a fine *crescendo* is obtained, preparing the entrance of the pedal. The principal section ends in the middle of measure 57.

On the second eighth before the last, in this measure, the right hand passes to the second manual, the left remaining on the great. In measures 60 and 61 the hands carry out the change so as to take the first descending run on the great-manual, and the second run on the second manual. But some players think it better to defer the employment of two manuals till later; they do not begin the change till measure 62, after having remained, from the second half of measure 59, on either the first or the second manual.

In measures 62 to 65 the first half of each measure is played on the great-manual, the second half on the second manual. The whole of measure 66 is played on the great. In measures 67 to 69 the first half of each is played on the second manual, the second half on the great.

In the first half of measure 70 the hands are still on the second manual; then the soprano goes over to the great, the left not following till the third quarter of measure 73. It may, however, already go over to the great-manual with the second sixteenth in the second quarter of measure 72.

On the second sixteenth in the third quarter of measure 73, draw the mixtures of the great-organ, so that the figurations in the succeeding measures may come out well in spite of the low range.

In what follows, alternate the manuals so as to execute the first half of each measure on the second manual, and the second half on the great.

It should be mentioned that some organists perform the section from the middle of measure 70 onward to the entrance of the figure in measure 73 (the one repeated by the echo) entirely on the second manual; but a simultaneous employment of two manuals is demanded by the notation, which indicates an interlacing of the parts at the beginning of measure 72.

After alternating between the two manuals up to the second half of measure 83, both hands remain on the great-manual from there onward. Utilize the low range in measures 83 and 84 for successively bringing on any mixture-stops not previously drawn.

On the first and third quarters of measure 85, and the first in measure 86, bring on the reeds in succession. Do not draw the 16-foot manual-stops yet.

Continue in this tone-power to the beginning of measure 97. At this point a prolonged *decrescendo* commences, which extends to measure 109, then being abruptly interrupted by the *fortissimo* entrance of the pedal.

The above *decrescendo* may be carried out in various ways, depending on the instrument and the player's taste. The following procedure is to be recommended. On the second eighth before the last in measure 97, and on both the third and the second eighths before the last in measure 98, throw off the great-organ reeds in succession. Here the retirement of these registers will hardly be noticed, because it has the effect of a sort of *diminuendo* on the suspensions. Before the last sixteenth in measure 99, after the third quarter in measure 100, and after the first quarter in measure 101, retire successively the mixtures of the great-organ, and also, if you like, the 2-foot and 4-foot foundation stops.

On the last eighth in measure 102 the two higher parts go over to the second manual, on which the mixtures and reeds are not thrown off; the swell-box still remains open. The left hand plays on the great-manual up to the third quarter in measure 105; from there onward both hands are on the second manual, and the swell closes gradually. In the meantime the mixtures and reeds of the great-organ will be drawn again.

The underlying idea in this mode of executing the *decrescendo* is, therefore, that it shall not finish with soft stops, but with the full tone of the second manual tempered only by the closing of the swell. This sounds to the listener as if the *fortissimo* were still continuing, but borne on into the distance and dying away, to revive in full splendor with the entrance of the pedal. In this way the *fortissimo* entrance of the pedal has a surprising, but not a harsh, effect. On the other hand, if it is made to break in upon the *pianissimo* of the softest stops, the passage is rendered meaningless. Nothing is left but an empty effect quite unrelated to the logic of the piece.

We shall not conceal the fact that there are players who do not approve of bringing in a *decrescendo* from measures 97–109. They regard it as a vicious modernization, and prefer to play this section through in an even-toned *forte*.

Their objection is not well-founded. True, Bach probably did not carry out the *decrescendo* in the manner described above; but he doubtless did conceive this section as an episode. He probably already changed over in measure 97 by transferring the left hand to the *Rückpositiv** on the second eighth of the measure, letting the right hand follow on the fourth eighth. From here he remained on the *Rückpositiv* until the entrance of the pedal; unless—which is likewise possible—he embraced the opportunity towards the close to pass to the third manual.

However, if we conceive the section as an episode, and if it presents itself musically as a *diminuendo*, there is no reason why we should abstain from bringing out this *diminuendo* by such means as the modern organ affords.

After performing measures 109 to 114 with full organ, throw off the reeds of manuals and pedal at the beginning of measure 115. Measures 115–119 will be played, with foundation stops and mixtures, on the first and second manuals in alternation, the first half of each measure being executed on the first manual, and the second half on the second. The manual-to-pedal couplers are thrown off; the swell-box is open.

Some organists are of the opinion that this reminiscence of the middle division of the fugue ought not to be performed on alternating manuals, because it forms a part of the final development pressing onward to the close, and the alternation of the manuals interrupts the grand flow of the sweeping tide. Despite the echo-passages, they like to play it wholly on the great-organ, fortifying their position with the fact that Bach has the pedal-part continue throughout. This point is well

* *Rückpositiv* is here equivalent to choir-manual.

taken. In any event the alternation is appropriate only when one has a strong second manual at his disposal.

During the course of measure 119 bring on your pedal reeds and the manual-to-pedal couplers again. The reeds on the manuals are added later, on the rest at the beginning of measure 120. On the second eighth in measure 126, the 16-foot manual-registers will be added.

Ought we to execute the Recitativo (measures 127–129) and the Presto (measures 133–136) on the first manual or on the second? The probabilities favor the former method; for with the other the transition to the chords is always too abrupt, and the effect consequently bad. For playing these runs it is a good plan to throw off the 16-foot manual stops. For the Adagissimo, however, they will be drawn; they are also brought into action on the last eighth in measure 136, and remain drawn to the close.

Perform the Recitativo rather slowly, and without varying the rhythm too freely; do not exaggerate the breadth of movement in the Adagissimo, or the liveliness of the Presto and Vivace. The impression on the hearer should be that of an inner unity between these movements, as they succeed one another in the Coda.

Edited by
Charles-Marie Widor
and Albert Schweitzer

Toccata and Fugue in D Minor

Johann Sebastian Bach

Toccata
Adagio

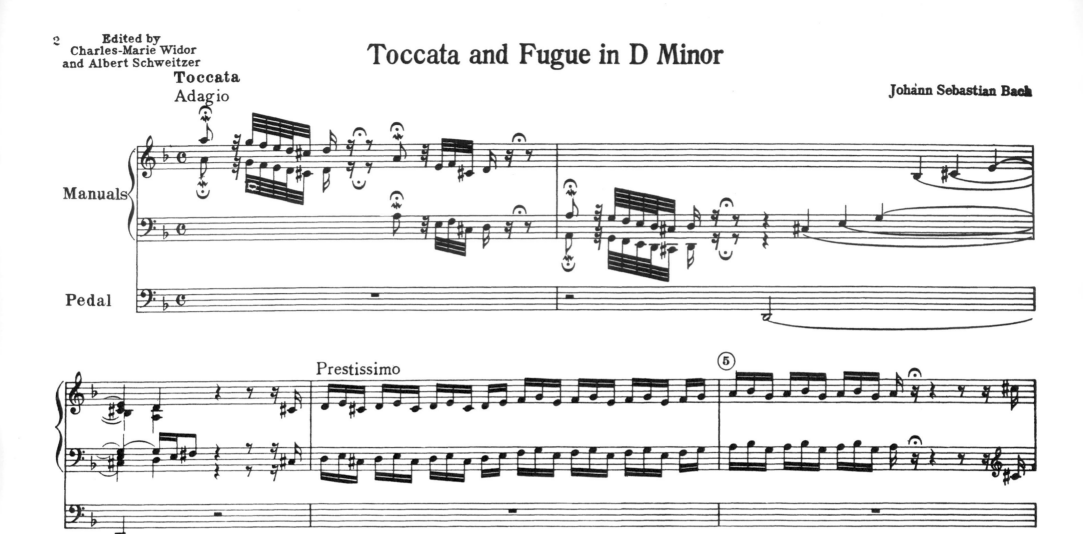

31144 X

4

Prestissimo

31144

Fugue

8

31144

Recitativo

Adagissimo

Presto

135

Adagio Vivace

140

Molto adagio

13

81144

0-73999-76040-8

0 73999 76040 8

HL50276040

G. SCHIRMER, Inc.

DISTRIBUTED BY

HAL•LEONARD®
CORPORATION

7777 W. BLUEMOUND RD. P.O. BOX 13819 MILWAUKEE, WI 53213

U.S. $9.99

ISBN 978-0-7935-5263-4

50999

9 780793 552634